WALKING
MEDITATION

Other programs by Thich Nhat Hanh available through Sounds True

Spoken Word Audio
Happiness, Love, and Liberation (2015)
Body and Mind Are One (2013)
Living Without Stress or Fear (2009)
Call Me By My True Names (2009)
The Essential Thich Nhat Hanh Collection
(compilation of *The Art of Mindful Living,*
Living Without Stress or Fear, and *Teachings on Love*) (2009)
Mindfulness and Psychotherapy (2005, 1998)
Touching the Earth with Sister Chân Không (2004)
Plum Village Meditations (2004)
Teachings on Love (2004, 1996)
The Ultimate Dimension (2004)
The Present Moment (2003, 1999, 1994)
Peacemaking (2002)
The Art of Mindful Living (2000, 1991)

Online Training Course
Body and Mind Are One (2012)

Music
Drops of Emptiness with Sister Chân Không (2007, 2003)

Video
Mindful Movements (2005)

EASY STEPS
TO MINDFULNESS

WALKING
MEDITATION

NGUYEN ANH-HUONG
& THICH NHAT HANH

sounds true
BOULDER, COLORADO

Sounds True
Boulder, CO 80306

Published 2006, 2019

Cover design & photo research by Lisa Kerans
Book design by Beth Skelley

Cover photo © Plum Village Community of Engaged Buddhism
Photos on pages v, x, 4, 15, 21, 30, 33, 34, 41, 46, 56, 63, 71, 81, 94, and all line art © Shutterstock
Photos on pages vii, 75, 101 © Don Farber
Photos on pages 16, 51, 55, 76, 80, 86, 92–93 © Paul Davis
Photo on pages 24 and 100 © Thu Nguyen

Printed in the United States of America

Library of Congress Cataloging-in-Publication Data
Names: Nguyen, Anh Huong, author. | Nhat Hanh, Thích, author.
Title: Walking meditation : easy steps to mindfulness / Nguyen Anh-Huong & Thich Nhat Hanh.
Description: Boulder, Colorado : Sounds True, [2019] | Includes bibliographical references
Identifiers: LCCN 2018019974 (print) | LCCN 2018042136 (ebook) | ISBN 9781591798828 (ebook) |
    ISBN 9781683642749 (pbk.)
Subjects: LCSH: Meditation—Buddhism. | Walking—Religious aspects—Buddhism.
Classification: LCC BQ5612 (ebook) | LCC BQ5612 .N44 2019 (print) | DDC 294.3/4435—dc23
LC record available at https://lccn.loc.gov/2018019974

10 9 8 7 6 5 4 3 2 1

Walking Meditation

Take my hand.
We will walk.
We will only walk.
We will enjoy our walk
without thinking of arriving anywhere.
Walk peacefully.
Walk happily.
Our walk is a peace walk.
Our walk is a happiness walk.

Then we learn
that there is no peace walk;
that peace is the walk;
that there is no happiness walk;
that happiness is the walk.
We walk for ourselves.
We walk for everyone
always hand in hand.

Walk and touch peace every moment.
Walk and touch happiness every moment.
Each step brings a fresh breeze.
Each step makes a flower bloom under our feet.
Kiss the Earth with your feet.
Print on Earth your love and happiness.

Earth will be safe
when we feel in us enough safety.

THICH NHAT HANH

CONTENTS

INTRODUCTION

Peace Is Every Step

Peace is every step.
The shining red sun is my heart.
Each flower smiles with me.
How green, how fresh all that grows.
How cool the wind blows.
Peace is every step.
It turns the endless path to joy.

TINH THUY
senior student of Thich Nhat Hanh

In the midst of our chaotic world, we tend to lose touch with the peace and joy that are available in each moment: the sunshine, the birds' singing, the autumn leaves, a baby's smile. The practice of walking meditation brings us back to being fully present and alive with every step, filling each moment with peace and joy.

Over the past four decades, my teacher, Zen Master Thich Nhat Hanh, has offered walking meditation practice to hundreds of thousands of people around the world. It has transformed many people's lives, including my own. I was introduced to the practice in 1980, and it has stayed with me and become my life. I have shared it with many people at mindfulness workshops and retreats at the Mindfulness Practice Center of Fairfax in Oakton, Virginia, and elsewhere.

This book includes a complete program of meditation instruction that you can use to create your own walking meditation practice. Be sure to read the instructions for each practice before listening to the guided session. You will also be instructed when to watch the video, which features archival footage of the Venerable Thich Nhat Hanh instructing students in the basic practice of slow walking meditation. All five guided audio meditations and the instructional video are found on the Walking Meditation page of the Sounds True website at SoundsTrue.com/walkingmeditation/meditations.

It is with great happiness that I share the art of mindful walking with you. If you follow this training program wholeheartedly, the value of your practice will be beyond measure. The boundary between practice and non-practice will eventually disappear, and every time you take a step, it will be a peaceful one. Every time you walk, it will be a walking meditation.

CONSCIOUS BREATHING MEDITATION

The Welcoming Path

The empty path welcomes you,
fragrant with grass and little flowers,
the path paved with paddy fields
still bearing the marks of your childhood
and the fragrance of mother's hand.
Walk leisurely, peacefully.
Your feet touch the Earth deeply.
Don't let your thoughts carry you away,
come back to the path every moment.
The path is your dear friend.
She will transmit to you
her solidity,
and her peace.

THICH NHAT HANH

Meditation is not meant to help us avoid problems or run away from difficulties. It is meant to allow positive healing to take place. To meditate is to learn how to stop—to stop being carried away by our regrets about the past, our anger or despair in the present, or our worries about the future. By practicing the art of stopping, we can enter the present moment and be nourished by the beauty and wonder of life in and around us: the smell of flowers, the warmth of sunshine, the color of the sky. To practice mindfulness is to begin to realize that we have a choice—to stop and rest or run, to be angry or happy. Once we choose to stop, everything will be okay.

Before learning walking meditation, we begin by learning how to breathe mindfully. This is the best way to help us learn to rest and stop. When we breathe and know that we are breathing, our wandering mind begins to rest on the pillow of our breath. A feeling of calm and ease then naturally arises.

The fundamental practice of conscious breathing meditation is to nourish your mindfulness and learn how to keep it present, alive, and strong. When you learn how to generate the energy of mindfulness and allow it to penetrate everything you do, understanding, compassion, and loving kindness will naturally flower in you. At the beginning you may think that you are practicing mindfulness only while walking, but then one morning you might make some tea; you pick up the mug and suddenly you can smell the tea more keenly than ever before. And as you take a sip, the tea becomes more delicious because the energy of mindfulness that you have developed allows you to taste it more directly and deeply.

Your breath is part of your body, so when your mind is in touch with your breath through mindful breathing, it is also in touch with your body. True rest and peace are the natural result of conscious breathing in which body, breath, and mind come into unity.

To practice basic conscious breathing meditation, sit comfortably and let your weight sink into the ground. You can also practice conscious breathing while standing, walking, or in any other position, or even while jogging. If you have physical limitations and cannot sit or stand comfortably, you can lie on your back. Whether you walk or jog, sit or stand, as long as you remain mindful of your breathing, peace and serenity are always with you.

Sit in such a way that you can enjoy each moment of your sitting. You can sit on a chair if sitting on a cushion is difficult for you. If you experience a lot of restlessness or resistance in your sitting, lie down instead.

Whether you are sitting or standing, keep your head and neck aligned with your spinal column by dropping your shoulders completely. If you are lying down, let your arms rest alongside your body at an angle that enables your shoulders to fully relax. Your hands can rest on your belly or on the floor. If you need to use a pillow, choose one that is thin enough to support your head without tensing your neck. To loosen your jaw, open your mouth as wide as you can three times, followed each time by a deep breath. Now, close your eyes and allow your facial muscles to relax completely by keeping a half-smile on your lips. A half-smile helps bring you back to the source of love, joy, and compassion within you. Let your breath flow naturally and allow the river of your breath to carry your gentle smile to every part of your body.

Your elbows and wrists should be loose. Relax each of your fingers. If you are sitting, you can place one hand on top of the other, interlock your fingers, or let your hands rest naturally on your lap.

When you feel settled in this sitting or lying position, put your hands on your belly and continue to breathe naturally. With your in-breath, allow all of your thoughts to move down to the level of your abdomen and settle there. As you breathe out, allow your whole body to feel softened and cleansed as tensions and stresses in your body are released. As you breathe in, quietly say "Resting" while allowing all of your mental activities to rest in your abdomen. Then, during the whole length of your out-breath, quietly say "Softening" as your body relaxes and becomes as soft as a baby's. Practice this exercise— breathing in, "Resting"; breathing out, "Softening"— for a few minutes or as long as you wish until you experience a sense of deep ease and calm.

Your mind has been resting on the soft pillow of your breath and because of that your breath has become deeper, quieter, and slower. Now, give your gentle and complete attention to your breathing and nothing else. Place your hands on your abdomen so you can feel it rise and fall with your in-breath and out-breath. Have you noticed that it rises as you breathe in and falls as you breathe out? This is healthy breathing. When we are tense or taken over by a strong emotion, our breathing becomes short and shallow, and our belly does not move at all.

Now, as you breathe in, follow the air that enters your body through your nose, feel the rise of your abdomen, and quietly say, "In, one." With your out-breath, feel the fall of your abdomen and quietly say, "Out, one." Say "In, two" on the second in-breath, and "Out, two" on the second out-breath. Continue for ten full breaths. Counting your breath in this way helps you to cultivate mindfulness and concentration, which are crucial for nourishing peace and happiness.

At first you may find it difficult to remain mindful for as many as ten breaths, but once you are able to take ten conscious breaths in a row, you can continue until you reach fifteen. And if you want to do more, you can continue until you reach twenty breaths. I will lead you through a basic Conscious Breathing Meditation practice in the first guided audio meditation.

Conscious Breathing Meditation

Now, sit comfortably, relaxingly. If you have some physical limitations and you cannot sit, you can lie down on your back. As we sit down, we let our weight sink into the ground. We keep our head and neck aligned with our spinal column by dropping our shoulders completely. Our face is relaxed. Our elbows, our wrists, are loose. Our ten fingers are completely relaxed. We can place one hand on top of the other, we can interlock our fingers, or we can just rest our hands on our lap, any way we like.

Now, we give our attention to our breathing. We breathe naturally, through our nose. As we breathe in, we know that we are breathing in. As we breathe out, we become fully aware of our out-

Listen to **Conscious Breathing Meditation** at SoundsTrue.com/walkingmeditation/meditations.

breath. This is to allow ourselves to just rest on the soft pillow of the breath. Breathing in, feel your in-breath. Breathing out, feel your out-breath. In, out. Relax your face. Relax your jaw. Relax and allow your chest to open.

Allow your abdomen to soften. You may like to use your hand and gently massage your chest, to be sure that your chest is relaxed. Use your hand to feel your tummy as your breath flows naturally in and out. If you find any tension anywhere in your chest, in your abdomen, in your body, put your hand there and allow your breath to move through the area where there is tension.

Your breath is like a fresh stream of water, a fresh breeze, moving through the area that is tense to help with dissolving the tension. And more importantly, let a half-smile come to your lips, so that your breath can carry your half-smile to the place where there is tension. We continue to breathe with a half-smile on our lips in this way until we feel completely relaxed.

Relax your shoulders. Breathing in, here is my in-breath. Breathing out, here comes my out-breath. In-breath, out-breath. In, out. With your hand on your tummy, can you feel how your abdomen rises with your in-breath and falls with your out-breath? Breathing in, abdomen expanding. Breathing out, abdomen contracting. Expanding, contracting. Rising, falling.

You begin to feel more relaxed than ever. You feel soft, soft. You feel fresh, and you are at peace. You are home. Breathing in, softening. Breathing out, nurturing. In, softening. Out, nurturing. In, being peace. Out, smiling to peace. Your breath continues to flow like a river, in and out.

Enjoy your breathing as long as you want.

If You Experience Difficulties Practicing Conscious Breathing Meditation

Although conscious breathing will eventually become very natural and enjoyable for you, it takes some effort at the beginning. But if you practice a short period of mindful breathing for ten breaths twice a day—after you wake up in the morning and before you go to bed at night—the practice will grow stronger in you over time. One day you will wake up and remember to breathe naturally, because you will have sown the seed of mindful breathing and watered it daily.

In meditation, the practice of calming, resting, and dwelling happily in the present moment can be difficult at first because our minds are always racing. The more you try to stop your racing mind, the more it resists. Mindfulness is not meant to suppress or get rid of the racing mind, but simply recognize its presence. First you need to acknowledge that thinking nonstop has become a strong habit for you. The easiest way to keep that habit from taking you over is to learn how to breathe in a sitting position for a short time, for just five or ten breaths. If you think you have to practice meditation for too long a period of time, there is no way you will maintain a daily practice. Instead, throughout the day you can use the ringing of the telephone or the sound of your watch or any other cue to stop all doing and thinking for a moment. Just enjoy your breathing. Our son started sitting when he was three or four years old. Before he went to kindergarten, he sat for ten breaths every morning. And if a little child can do that, I am sure we grown-ups can do that as well.

If anxiety, sorrow, confusion, or fear happen to arise while you sit, greet them with a gentle smile; and if you are a visual person, invite them to rest in your lap or next to you as you sit. Return to the practice of conscious breathing: "Breathing in, I feel (or rest on, or smile to) my in-breath"; "Breathing out, I feel (or rest on, or smile to) my out-breath." Practicing in this way will help calm both your body and your emotions, and as a result you will begin to experience the peace and joy of sitting.

There is a wisdom inside of us that tells us what to do at certain moments. We can wake up that wisdom through meditation practice until, eventually, the process becomes quite natural for us and takes place on a subconscious level.

If you think that peace and happiness are somewhere else and you run after them, you will never arrive. It is only when you realize that peace and happiness are available here in the present moment that you will be able to relax.

In daily life, there is so much to do and so little time. You may feel pressured to run all the time. Just stop! Touch the ground of the present moment deeply, and you will touch real peace and joy.

T.N.H.

2

SLOW WALKING
MEDITATION

Walking meditation is meditation while walking.
We walk slowly, in a relaxed way, keeping a
light smile on our lips. When we practice this
way, we feel deeply at ease, and our steps
are those of the most secure person on Earth.
All our sorrows and anxieties drop away, and
peace and joy fill our hearts. Anyone can do it.
It takes only a little time, a little mindfulness,
and the wish to be happy.   **THICH NHAT HANH**

You have just learned how to stop and rest in a sitting or lying position. You will now learn how to stop, rest, and become fully present and alive as you walk. This is called walking meditation, or mindful walking.

The primary purpose of walking meditation is to completely enjoy the experience of walking. We walk all the time, but usually our walking is more like running. Our steps are often burdened with our anxieties and sorrows. When we walk in forgetfulness, we imprint our anxieties and sorrows on Mother Earth and on those around us. But when we walk in mindfulness, each step creates a fresh breeze of peace, joy, and harmony.

When we practice walking meditation, we do not try to arrive anywhere or attain any particular goal. Our destination is the here and now. The Buddha said, "The past no longer is. The future has not yet come. Looking deeply at life as it is in the very here and now, the practitioner dwells in stability and freedom." We do not put something in front of us and run after it, because everything we have been looking for—peace, joy, love, transformation, healing, enlightenment—can only be found inside us in the present moment. Where are we going? Why do we need to hurry? Where is our final destination? These are questions that help us to put things into perspective so that we know where we are and where we want to go from here.

We may believe that we can do anything except return to the present moment because we fear that the pain in the present moment is unbearable. Deep inside us we harbor the belief that there is nothing else in the present moment besides despair, confusion, and suffering. Please ask the Earth, the trees, the birds, the sunshine, and friends who are already on this path of mindfulness practice to help you make this gentle, loving step without struggle. You will learn that the air, the trees, the birds, and the flowers are always there for you. Each time you take a mindful step, you are back in the arms of Mother Earth and are reminded of your true, sweet home in the here and now.

When people come to practice with us, we always begin every day with a short sitting meditation, some mindful stretching, and a slow, mindful walk. By beginning each day this way, our students find peace, joy, love, and stability, and these qualities permeate the rest of their day. They learn that the practice works, and since it works, they will continue it. You have to taste it first before you know whether or not you want to continue. Once you taste it and then miss it when you do not have it, you will feel the need to return to the practice.

Whenever you do slow walking indoors, I recommend that you take off your shoes. You can feel the floor and connect with the Earth more easily without shoes. The flow between you and Mother Earth then becomes stronger. The longer you practice walking with this connection, the more your heart will be softened and opened, and the more you will feel nurtured, solid, and taken care of by the Earth. Once again, do not start with an unrealistic goal, such as practicing for an hour or so. But if you can take one peaceful step, you can take two, three, four, or more. In the second guided audio meditation, I will teach you how to coordinate the conscious breathing

In Buddhism, there is a word, "apranihita." It means wishlessness or aimlessness. The idea is that we do not put anything ahead of ourselves and run after it. When we practice walking meditation, we walk in this spirit. We just enjoy the walking, with no particular aim or destination. Our walking is not a means to an end. We walk for the sake of walking.

A.J. Muste said, "There is no way to peace, peace is the way." Walking in mindfulness brings us peace and joy, and makes our life real. Why rush? Our final destination will only be the graveyard. Why not walk in the direction of life, enjoying peace in each moment with every step? There is no need to struggle. Enjoy each step. We have already arrived.

T.N.H.

you have learned in the previous chapter with your steps. As you continue to walk and breathe in this way, the process of softening and nurturing will take place in you, and your heart will begin to open to life, to all that is. You will feel nurtured every time your foot kisses the floor or the Earth as the solidity of the Earth springs up into your body and heart. You will also learn how to silently say certain words in your heart as you walk, and you will find yourself naturally becoming more kind, loving, and peaceful.

We can practice walking meditation by counting steps or by using words. If the rhythm of our breathing is three steps for each in-breath and out-breath (3-3), for example, we can say, silently, "Lotus flower blooms. Lotus flower blooms," or "The green planet. The green planet," as we walk. If our breathing is two steps for each in-breath, and three steps for each out-breath

Watch the **Walking Meditation** video at SoundsTrue.com/walkingmeditation/meditations.

(2-3), we might say, "Lotus flower. Lotus flower blooms." Or "Walking on the green planet. Walking on the green planet," for 5-5. Or "Walking on the green planet, I'm walking on the green planet," for 5-6.

We don't just say the words. We really see flowers blooming under our feet. We really become one with our green planet. Feel free to use your own creativity and wisdom. Walking meditation is not hard labor. It is for your enjoyment. **THICH NHAT HANH**

Feel free to use your own creativity and wisdom.
Walking meditation is not hard labor.
It is for your enjoyment.

T.N.H.

Slow Walking Meditation

Stand relaxingly, just like with the sitting. We let our weight sink deeply into the ground, so that we can see ourselves as trees, with our deep roots in the Earth.

Again, please keep your head and neck aligned with your spine, by dropping your shoulders. Loosen your hips. Flex your knees. Loosen your elbows, your wrists. Relax.

Please breathe calmly with your belly, like we did during our sitting. Do you still feel the rise of your abdomen with your in-breath? And the fall of your abdomen with your out-breath? Is the gentle baby smile still on your lips, on your face? Wonderful.

Now, press your feet firmly on the ground. Shift your weight to your left foot, so that you can feel that you're sinking into the left foot, into the ground, and the right leg is empty of weight. Continue to breathe calmly.

Listen to **Slow Walking Meditation** at SoundsTrue.com/walkingmeditation/meditations.

Now, shift your weight to your right leg. Can you feel the contact between the sole of your right foot and the floor?

Now, let's begin slow walking. We'll begin with our left foot. Now, as we breathe in, we bring our left foot forward and place it down on the floor. So, one inhalation, one step. As we breathe out, we lift our right foot up, we bring it forward, and we place it down on the floor.

So, one inhalation, one step; one exhalation, one step. Relax. Relax your shoulders. Relax your face.

Let's continue: breathing in, one step, breathing out, one step. As we breathe in, we feel the rise of our abdomen and we place our foot on the floor. As we breathe out, we feel the fall of our abdomen, as we make the next step. You may like to put one or both hands on your tummy as you walk.

So, your mind is with your breath and your step at the same time. Breathe in. One step. Breathe out. One step. Feel your weight being shifted from one leg to another. Be fully aware of the contact between the sole of your foot and the floor—the foot that is making the step. When the contact between the sole of our foot and the floor is perfect, we are fully present.

You may experience some imbalance, if this is the first time you practice slow walking. Just allow your weight to sink into the ground. Continue to relax. Breathing in, one gentle step; breathing out, one gentle step. In, out. Stepping, stepping. Stepping, stepping. Breathing in, breathing out.

Please continue to walk in this way. Your eyes are half open, looking down in front of you at an angle that does not bend your neck. So, your neck is still relaxed, your head is sitting relaxingly on your neck. Upright, with very relaxing posture. Your eyes are looking down but it's a soft-eye look. We don't try to capture anything in particular. The soft eye, the gentle step, the belly breathing, and the half smile that is holding all of this together.

Our mind is at the sole of our foot. When our foot kisses the Earth, kisses the floor, our mind also kisses the floor, kisses the Earth. The mind, the breath, the step, the gentle baby smile, all become one as we walk in this way. Our anxieties, our worries, our sorrow, stop and rest with every step we make, with every breath that comes and goes.

Now, we can hold words in our heart as we walk. Holding words in our heart as we walk can help us to be more focused, more present, more concentrated, as we walk. What is happening when we make a step like this with an in-breath? We stop, right? We have arrived. We don't have the need to go forward, to run after anything. We become fully present. We feel at home. The Earth is our mother. The Earth is our home. This moment is our home. This body, this breath, is our home.

So, we can say quietly, in our heart, "I have arrived. I am home." When we make a step with an in-breath, we say quietly in our heart, "I have arrived." As we make the next step with an out-breath, we say, "I am home." Breathing in, one step, "I have arrived." Breathing out, one step, "I am home." "I have arrived." "I am home." Arrived. Home. Arrived. Home.

Where is home? In the here, in the now. So, as we breathe in, making one step, we can say, quietly, "In the here." "In the now," as we breathe out, and make another step. Breathing in, one step, "In the here." Breathing out, one step, "In the now." "In the here." "In the now." Here. Now. Here. Now. I have arrived. I am home. In the here. In the now. Here. Now.

Please continue walking in this way, holding words in your heart, to help you stay present continuously with your steps. Breathing in, one step, and say to yourself, "Relaxed," as you breathe in, and smile to the feeling of relaxation in you as you breathe out, and make the next step.

Our heart begins to open to life, to all that is, and suddenly, we feel nurtured. Every time our foot kisses the floor, the Earth, the energy of love, the solidity from the Earth springs up into our body and mind. Breathing in, nurturing. Breathing out, nurturing. So, every step we make, we're not just touching and kissing the Earth superficially, but we are connecting deeply with Mother Earth. And because of that, we feel nurtured, and nurturing is healing.

And you can walk in this way as long as you wish.

If You Have Difficulty with Slow Walking Meditation

If you experience a lot of difficulty in your practice of sitting and walking meditation, it is best to practice lying-down meditation for about five or ten minutes before you begin. While lying down, become fully aware of your body from the top of your head to the tips of your fingers and toes as you breathe in, and smile to your whole body as you breathe out. Keep in mind that the air you breathe in is a gift coming to you from the whole universe—this can

When you begin to practice walking meditation, you might feel unbalanced, like a baby learning to walk. Follow your breathing, dwell mindfully on your steps, and soon you will find your balance. Visualize a tiger walking slowly, and you will find that your steps become as majestic as the steps of a tiger.

T.N.H.

help you feel deeply nourished and refreshed every time you breathe in.

Once again, it is important not to set unrealistic goals. You can begin your walking practice by saying, "I will take ten steps, and ten steps only." Allow yourself to relax into your breathing and your steps. Take one step with one breath at a time. If you can take one peaceful step, you can take another, and another. Place your mind at the sole of the foot as you step. When your foot kisses the Earth, your mind also kisses the Earth.

When people come to their first mindfulness retreat, they often feel tired at the beginning. They have doubts about whether the practice will work for them. But as the retreat goes on, they always feel stronger, lighter, and happier. When our minds cannot stop thinking, we do not realize how tired and emotional we may be. For this reason, when you begin the daily practice of mindful walking, you may feel a little emotionally unstable. Not to worry! Just keep practicing.

If you have difficulty maintaining your balance while practicing slow walking, it is understandable because the only time you previously walked slowly was when you were a toddler. Be patient! These difficulties will pass once you become used to mindful walking and begin to enjoy it. Imagine for a moment that this morning was the first time you got out of bed and started standing and walking after being bedridden for many months. You will see that it is a great miracle to be able to stand upright and take steps on the Earth. You will deeply savor every step you take.

3

WALKING MEDITATION IN NATURE

The practice of walking meditation opens your eyes to the wonders and the suffering of the universe. If you are not aware of what is going on around you, where do you expect to encounter ultimate reality?

Every path can be a walking meditation path, from tree-lined roadsides and fragrant rice paddies to the back alleys of Mostar and the mine-filled dirt roads of Cambodia. When you are awake, you will not hesitate to enter any path.

You will suffer, not just from your own worries and fears, but because of your love for all beings. When you open yourself in this way, your companions will be other beings on the path of awakening who share your insight. They will work with you, side by side, to alleviate the world's suffering. **THICH NHAT HANH**

One morning when my son was two years old, I put him in his stroller and took him for a walk. As we were walking, the songs of birds filled the air. When he heard their songs, he opened his eyes widely, looked up, smiled, and said, "Yes! Yes!"

We were all children once. We said yes to the birds calling. To practice mindful walking is to learn how to become a child again, to smile again to the birds, to the sunshine, to the rain. To say yes to the birds, to say yes to life. When you practice walking meditation in this way for a few days, saying yes, you will undergo a deep transformation and learn how to enjoy peace in each moment of your life.

Your mind is like a piece of land planted with many different kinds of seeds: seeds of joy, peace, mindfulness, understanding, and love; seeds of craving, anger, fear, hate, and forgetfulness. These wholesome and unwholesome seeds are always there, sleeping in the soil of your mind. The quality of your life depends on which seeds you water. If you plant tomato seeds in your garden, tomatoes will grow. Just so, if you water a seed of peace in your mind, peace will grow. When the seed of happiness in you is watered, you will become happy. When the seed of anger in you is watered, you will become angry. The seeds that are watered frequently are those that will grow strong.

When I am in nature, I often like to smile and say hello to what I see, hear, and come into contact with. I learn to smile to a pebble that I happen to step on. I smile to the blue sky, to the geese, to the leaves rustling in the wind, to an acorn falling on the ground, to the sight of mist rising from the grass in early morning. With my half-smile, I can feel my breath and my steps more clearly, recognize any tension in my face and body, and relax.

Sometimes it is difficult to relax into the breath and surrender at each step without the half-smile. But once you learn to smile to your breath and your steps, you will be able to smile to your joy, and eventually to your pain.

By coordinating your breathing with your steps, you establish yourself fully in the present moment, and your senses become empowered with the energy of mindfulness. You learn to say hello to what you see, hear, step on, and pass as you walk outside in nature. You can say hello quietly in your heart, or you can say hello out loud if you are alone and feel comfortable doing so. For example, if you hear the birds singing as you walk, you can say hello to them quietly in your heart.

During outdoor walking practice, in order to connect more deeply with all of the healing elements within and around you, you may want to stop walking from time to time and simply breathe. The more you make yourself available to these elements, the more you are refreshed and healed. You may enjoy this exercise, "Breathing in, good morning, birds"; "Breathing out, thank you for your songs," or "Breathing in, hello blue sky"; "Breathing out, thank you, dear blue sky, for being there for me." When you can make yourself more present in this way, the birds and the blue sky are yours to enjoy and hold. If you continue to breathe consciously and smile to the sky, its space and beauty begin to penetrate your whole being, nourishing you and waking within you the seeds of joy, love, and freedom. And during this time, you will refrain from watering the seeds of sorrow, anger, and despair.

Doing walking meditation in this way also helps us mend our hearts. Life has not been easy for many of us, and oftentimes our hearts have been torn and broken. But as we learn to walk mindfully, coming home to the Earth with each step, we mend our broken hearts. Every step you take in this spirit becomes a healing stitch that mends the places in you that are wounded.

Once you are accustomed to linking your breath with your steps during slow indoor walking, you can coordinate your breath with your steps when you walk outside by counting the number of steps you take with each inhalation and exhalation. At the beginning, allow your whole body to relax into each step as you walk slowly and feel the natural rhythm of your breathing. After five or ten minutes, see how many steps you can take with your in-breath, and how many steps with your out-breath. The number of steps you take with each breath depends on the rhythm of your breathing and your pace. You might take three steps with your in-breath and three steps with your out-breath. If your in-breath is two-and-a-half steps long and your out-breath is two-and-a-half steps long, then you could walk a littler faster, so that you take three steps for each breath. Or you could walk a little slower so you take two steps for each breath. Silently say "In" with each step as you breathe in, and "Out" with each step as you breathe out. If for example your in-breath is three steps long, silently say "In, in, in" with the in-breath and "Out, out, out" with the out-breath. If you want to connect deeply with the Earth and feel as solid as the Earth, then silently say "Earth, Earth, Earth" while you breathe in, and "Solid, solid, solid" while you breathe out. Or you can say "Arrived, arrived, arrived," and "Home, home, home." Feel free to use words that help you feel calm, solid, and at ease as you walk.

I will lead you through a session of "Walking Meditation in Nature" in the third guided audio meditation.

If you see something along the way that you want to touch with your mindfulness—the blue sky, the hills, a tree, or a bird—just stop, but while you do, continue breathing mindfully. You can keep the object of your contemplation alive by means of mindful breathing. If you don't breathe consciously, sooner or later your thinking will settle back in, and the bird or the tree will disappear. Always stay with your breathing.

T.N.H.

Walking Meditation in Nature

We begin with a moment of standing like a tree. Feeling our deep, quiet breaths, and our connection with the Earth beneath our feet.

Now, breathe normally. Three steps for each in-breath, three steps for each out-breath. Your breath may be longer or shorter than mine, depending on your lungs' needs. Please feel free to adjust your pace. Breathe and walk accordingly. For now, three steps with the inhalation, three steps with an exhalation. In, in, in. Relaxingly. Out, out, out. Joyfully. In, in, in. Out, out, out. We are caressing the Earth with our feet. Gentle steps, loving steps. Let's continue to breathe and walk joyfully. Our tummy is still going up gradually with our in-breath, going down naturally with our out-breath as we make steps: three steps with the in-breath, three steps for the out-breath.

Listen to **Walking Meditation in Nature** at SoundsTrue.com/walkingmeditation/meditations.

The air is so fresh. Ah, can you hear something? It's the birds calling, the birds calling us. Their songs are like a bell of mindfulness, calling us back home to this moment. What is happening in this moment? You and I, we are holding hands. We're still breathing. We're walking peacefully. We are still alive. The people we love are still alive. The leaves are dancing in the wind. Why don't we stop walking? As we hear the bird's calling, we want to listen to her call, deeply. She is calling us home, and we responded to her call by smiling gently and by breathing in and breathing out deeply. Breathing in, I have arrived. Breathing out, I am home.

We have already stopped walking. We're standing here, deeply rooted in the body of Earth. Saying silently, "I have arrived," with the in-breath; "I am home," with the out-breath. I have arrived. I am home. Breathing in, I feel relaxed. Breathing out, I am at peace. We are still standing here, feeling completely refreshed, completely softened up. Our heart is completely opened, like a child.

We now experience a sense of new opening. A sense

of spaciousness and joy of being alive. You see the grass becomes greener. The sky becomes clearer. We should continue to breathe consciously, and smile. Smiling as a way of saying, "Hello." We smile to the grass. We smile to the pebbles. We smile to the leaves beneath our steps. To the flowers. To the fresh breeze that is kissing our cheeks. We smile to the pines rustling in the wind. To the sunshine.

In order to continue allowing ourselves to be nourished by these wonders of life, let us continue our walk. Stepping, stepping, stepping. Three steps for the in-breath. Smiling, smiling, smiling. Three steps for the out-breath. Breathing in. Breathing out. Breathing in, we can say silently, "Yes, yes, yes." Breathing out, silently we say, "Yes, yes, yes." Breathing in, "Present moment." Breathing out, "Wonderful moment." If you like to say one word with each step, then you can say "Present, present, present," with the in-breath. And "Wonderful, wonderful, wonderful," for the out-breath.

Let's enjoy walking in silence.

After you have been practicing for a few days, try adding one more step to your exhalation. For example, if your normal breathing is 2-2, without walking any faster, lengthen your exhalation and practice 2-3 for four or five times. Then go back to 2-2.

In normal breathing, we never expel all the air from our lungs. There is always some left. By adding another step to your exhalation, you will push out more of this stale air. Don't overdo it. Four or five times are enough. More can make you tired. After breathing this way four or five times, let your breath return to normal. Then, five or ten minutes later, you can repeat the process. Remember to add a step to the exhalation, not the inhalation.

After practicing for a few more days, your lungs might say to you, "If you could do 3-3 instead of 2-3, that would be wonderful." If the message is clear, try it, but even then, only do it four or five times. Then go back to 2-2. In five or ten minutes, begin 2-3, and then do 3-3 again.

After several months, your lungs will be healthier and your blood will circulate better. Your way of breathing will have been transformed.   **THICH NHAT HANH**

4

WALKING MEDITATION
IN PUBLIC PLACES

You can practice walking meditation between meetings, on the way to your car, up or down stairs. When you walk anywhere, allow enough time to practice. Instead of three minutes, give yourself eight or ten. I always leave for the airport an extra hour early, so I can practice walking meditation there. Friends want to keep me until the last minute, but I resist. I tell them that I need the time. **THICH NHAT HANH**

You have learned the practice of slow walking indoors by walking quietly, taking one step with each breath. You have also learned how to walk as you hold words in your heart, and how to practice walking meditation outdoors in nature. Now, you will learn how to bring walking meditation into the day-to-day world by practicing it in public areas.

Once you taste the peace, joy, and serenity that result from the practice of slow, mindful walking indoors and in nature, you can practice walking meditation wherever you are. You can enjoy the steps between business meetings, or walking from the parking lot to your office, or in the subway, or at the airport. It is important that you allow enough time to walk so you do not have to rush and can enjoy walking without arriving anywhere, except in the present moment.

When you do walking meditation in a busy city, you can walk in the same way that you walk in nature. Feel free to coordinate your breathing with your steps to set a comfortable pace. There are many more sounds and sights, but through mindful breathing and walking you can create a refuge for yourself, a little island of peace amid the noise and confusion. You may not find as many beautiful, nurturing elements as you do in nature, but that does not prevent you from caressing the Earth with your feet; it does not prevent you from enjoying your breathing with your steps. The peaceful refuge that is created by the practice of mindful breathing and walking can be with you wherever you are.

When you are fully established in the present moment, your senses become empowered with the energy of mindfulness, and you can become more aware of your needs. You may be able to hear a message coming from your body about your need to relax. When the energy around you is chaotic, disturbing, or unsettled, you will naturally feel the need to be calm and relaxed. When you hear your body's message, you can hold the words "relaxing and calming" in your heart as you continue to walk and breathe. It is perfectly fine if you just want to feel your breathing and your steps without using words. Or feel free to silently say any other words that can help to make your steps more enjoyable.

Wherever you are, walk mindfully, arriving with each step you take, feeling the relaxation that comes with belly breathing. If you can synchronize your steps with your breath, do that. Otherwise, just let it all go. Come back to your heart, come back to your deep desire to relax, to be centered and calm. Allow your breath and your steps to flow naturally. As long as you can feel the solid Earth beneath your feet, your heart will remain open and you will feel your connection with the Earth and with all life.

When practicing mindful walking in public places, always breathe normally. Walk slowly, but not too slowly, because you do not want others to think you are too unusual. Walk a little slower than your normal pace, and a little faster than indoor walking. In this way you can enjoy peace and serenity as you walk without making the people around you uncomfortable.

I will lead you through a session of "Walking Meditation in Public Areas" in the fourth guided audio meditation.

Don't forget to practice smiling.

T.N.H.

Walking Meditation in Public Places

We begin with a moment of standing like a tree. Feeling our deep, quiet breaths and our connection with the Earth beneath our feet.

Now, three steps for each in-breath, three steps for each out-breath. Your breath may be longer or shorter than mine, depending on your lungs' needs. Please feel free to adjust your pace. Breathe and walk accordingly. If you take three steps when you breathe in, then say silently, "In, in, in." If you take three steps when you breathe out, then say silently, "Out, out, out." If your out-breath is four steps, then you can say, "Out, out, out, out." In, in, in. Out, out, out, out. We breathe in, we make three steps. In, in, in. We breathe out, we make three steps. Out, out, out.

Once your breathing and your steps have come together harmoniously, you may like to hold words in your heart while you walk, just as we did with the indoor slow walking. For example, we can

Listen to **Walking Meditation in Public Places** at SoundsTrue.com/walkingmeditation/meditations.

say silently as we breathe in, making three steps, "Relaxing, relaxing, relaxing." And as we breathe out, "Calming, calming, calming." It will also be perfectly fine if you just like to quietly enjoy the feeling of peace and serenity of outdoor walking without holding any words in your heart. In, in, in. Out, out, out. We breathe in, we make three steps. "In, in, in." We breathe out, we make three steps. "Out, out, out." Breathing in, step, step, step. Breathing out, step, step, step. Breathing in, relaxing, relaxing, relaxing. Breathing out, smiling, smiling, smiling.

Let's continue to enjoy our steps. Please do not forget your gentle smile.

When you begin to practice, your exhalation may be longer than your inhalation. You might find that you take three steps during your in-breath and four steps on your out-breath (3-4), or two steps/three steps (2-3). If this is comfortable for you, please enjoy practicing this way. After you have been doing walking meditation for some time, your in-breath and out-breath will probably become equal: 3-3, or 2-2, or 4-4.

Don't forget to practice smiling. Your half-smile will bring calm and delight to your steps and your breath, and help sustain your attention. After practicing for half an hour or an hour, you will find that your breath, your steps, your counting, and your half-smile all blend together in a marvelous balance of mindfulness.

The air is cleanest in the early morning and late evening. That is the best time to enjoy walking meditation. Allow the energy of that pure air to enter you.

When you practice walking meditation in the morning, your movements will become smooth and your mind will become alert. You will be more aware of what you are doing all day long. In making decisions, you will find that you are more calm and clear, that you have more insight and compassion. With each peaceful step you take, all beings, near and far, will benefit.   **THICH NHAT HANH**

With each peaceful step you take,
all beings, near and far, will benefit.

T.N.H.

5

WALKING MEDITATION
TO EMBRACE
YOUR EMOTIONS

There are two dimensions to life: the historical dimension, in which you identify with birth and death, ups and downs, beginnings and endings; and the ultimate dimension, where you see clearly that all of these are only concepts. As your solidity and freedom grow stronger, you begin to touch the ground of your being, which is the ultimate dimension of reality, and the door of no birth and no death opens.

The image often used for the two dimensions of life is that of water and waves. On the ocean's surface, there are many waves—some high, some low, some beautiful, and some less beautiful. All of them have a beginning and an end. But when you touch the waves deeply, you realize that waves are made only of water, and, from the point of view of the water, there is no beginning, no end, no up, no down, no birth, and no death.

When you touch the water—the ground of being—deeply, you can practice the last line of the verse: "In the ultimate, I dwell." As you breathe in, say, "Ultimate" with each step, and as you breathe out, say, "I dwell." These are not just words. If you really practice them, you will touch the world of no birth and no death with every step. **THICH NHAT HANH**

We do not practice mindful walking to eradicate our pain. We use the energy of mindfulness to be in better contact with our feelings and emotions, and to learn how to accept them. Your pain is not outside of you. It is a part of you, but it is never all of you. Suffering is always trying to emerge. If you do not have a way to listen to it and take care of it, you will instead keep yourself occupied or deny it. And if you try to suppress your suffering and your emotions, you will create stagnation in your psyche. You will not feel well and you may even become physically ill. You do not need to be afraid of your pain when mindfulness is there to embrace and transform it.

By practicing mindful breathing and walking, both your mind and body will naturally become lighter, calmer, and clearer. It is the same with your emotions. When your breathing is deep and relaxed, it will help to calm your feelings. And as you continue to breathe and walk mindfully, the energy of mindfulness will penetrate, embrace, and calm your pain until it softens. Then you can smile to your painful emotions, neither clinging to them nor rejecting them.

When you practice slow walking meditation or outdoor walking in nature, you have already begun the practice of allowing your pain, fear, and strong emotions to rest. Resting creates an environment for healing. If we cannot rest, we cannot heal. With continued mindfulness practice, you can create a peaceful space in your heart in which you can consciously embrace your feelings and emotions as you walk.

Do not try the practice of directly embracing your emotions before mastering the art of slow, mindful indoor walking and walking in nature. If you find that your emotions are ever too painful for you to cradle, return to the practice of slow walking meditation and conscious breathing in order to rest your mind and body and experience their natural calming effects. With continued practice, you will eventually become more capable of sipping the delicious water of compassion that lives in your heart.

When Strong Emotions Arise and Your Mindfulness Is Not Yet Strong Enough to Embrace Them

If emotions happen to come up during walking meditation at a time when your mindfulness is not strong enough to directly embrace them, simply recognize them by saying hello and smiling to them as you allow them to rest with each breath and each step. Please remember that your breath is the safest anchor. When you look at a tree in a storm, you see that its upper branches move violently in the wind. But if you look at its trunk, you see that it is very solid and still. Your belly is the trunk of your being. It is important to remember to allow everything in your head to move down to your abdomen. Put your hands on your abdomen and just practice belly breathing. After five, ten, or fifteen minutes, the storm will pass and you will be okay. Continue with daily sitting and walking practices until you can take hold of your emotions and care for them.

When our pain is big and we feel fragile, our safest course is indirect embracing. That is, we choose to spend as much time as possible in an environment that is conducive to the practice of mindfulness—in an environment where we can stop and water the seeds of joy, peace, compassion, and happiness. By living in this way, we let our peace and joy become a lullaby for our baby of pain. You do not need to be afraid of your pain, grief, or anger if your mindfulness is there to embrace and take care of these emotions. Your pain is your baby, your fear is your baby, and even your anger is your baby. If you can embrace unpleasant feelings with care, tenderness, and nonviolence, you can transform them into understanding and compassion.

When Mindfulness Is Stronger and We Choose to Invite Our Pain to Walk with Us

When unpleasant feelings or strong emotions arise while you are practicing walking meditation and you begin to feel some tension or pain in your body, you may feel the need to stop walking. Practice conscious breathing while lying down, sitting, or walking slowly, following the instructions given in chapters 1 and 2. Try to locate the tension or pain. Some of us hold pain in our chests, some in our stomachs or shoulders, and some in other areas of the body. Allow your breath and the energy of mindfulness to move through the pain, to relax and calm it. Then continue to walk and breathe while carrying your pain as you would a baby.

When a baby cries, his or her mother stops everything she is doing and picks the baby up. She does not need to ask her baby to be quiet. She usually only needs to hold the baby to calm and soothe him or her because the mother's energy is the energy of love, care, and tenderness. In the same way, it can sometimes be enough to merely hold the baby of your pain as you walk.

Breathing in,
I know that anger
is in me.
Breathing out,
I know this feeling
is unpleasant.

T.N.H.

As you continue to practice conscious breathing and walking, the energy of mindfulness will gradually penetrate and calm the pain or difficult emotion. Continue to walk and kiss the Earth with each step and breathe deeply into your belly, and remember to keep a half-smile on your lips. When you walk in this way, the baby of emotion calms, cools, and softens, and you will experience relief. You will find that you have made it safely through the storm.

It is the nature of strong emotion to come, stay for a while, and then go away. If you can remember that whenever a strong emotion or pain arises, you can embrace it with the energy of mindfulness—with mindful breathing and with mindful walking—then it will gradually lose its intensity. In meditation, the breath, the body, and the mind become one. And each one influences the other two. When your breath is calm and deep, your mind becomes calm and your body becomes relaxed. With continued practice of breathing, walking, and smiling, the energy of mindfulness will continue to penetrate, embrace, and calm your mental or physical pain until it becomes softer and lighter.

It may not be entirely pleasant at first to embrace your fear, pain, or grief, but with mindfulness you can hold them as a mother holds her crying baby, and you can feel safe even when the storm of strong emotions moves through you and out into the air and the Earth. To return to your breathing and your steps in difficult times is to remember that there is a solid mountain within you—it is as firm as the Earth beneath your feet—and to realize that you are more solid and resilient than you think.

It is a relief to be able to calm our pain, but that is not enough. The Buddha said that everything needs food to survive. You have to understand the makeup of your pain in order to choose not supply it with the nutrients that make it grow. To do that, you must train yourself in how to live your daily life as mindfully as possible, so that when the baby of pain needs a cradle, your energy of mindfulness will be strong enough to embrace it until you understand its roots. Once you come to understand how your pain is created, your emotions will give you new insights into your life, which will allow transformation and healing to take place.

You can practice indoor slow walking as you embrace your emotions. Or, if you like, you can go into your backyard, to the park, or to a riverbank where there are not very many people around you, and you can practice slow walking comfortably. I will lead you through a session of "Walking Meditation to Embrace Your Emotions" in the fifth guided audio meditation.

Walking Meditation to Embrace Your Emotions

You begin this practice in the standing position. Place your hands on your chest. As you return to your natural breathing, please begin to make steps with your breathing. One breath, one step, like we did for the slow indoor walking practice. Breathing in. One step. Say silently to yourself, "I feel uneasy." Breathing out. One step. Say silently, "I recognize that feeling in me."

When I say, "Breathing in," you breathe in and you make one step. You feel the contact between the sole of your foot and the floor, or the grass. When I say, "Breathing out," you breathe out as you make one step, feeling the contact between the sole of your foot and the ground.

Breathing in, "I feel uneasy." Say it silently to yourself. Breathing out, "I recognize that I am feeling uneasy." Breathing in, feeling uneasy. Breathing out, recognizing unease. In. I still feel uneasy. Out. It's OK. In. Unease. Out. It's OK.

Please keep walking, breathing, practicing in this way. As you breathe in, allow yourself to be present with your uneasy feeling. As you breathe out, say to yourself, "It's OK to feel this way." In. One step. Feeling uneasy. Out. One step. It is OK to feel this way. Relax your shoulders. Relax your face. And if you can, smile gently to this feeling of unease in you right now as you walk and breathe.

Breathing in, breathing out. Breathing in, you may begin to feel the fear, the anger, or the loneliness in you. Breathing out, you begin to feel that fear, anger, loneliness begin to come up in you.

Breathing in, say hello to your fear, anger, loneliness that is arising in you. Breathing out, say hello to your emotion. Keep breathing and stepping, relaxingly.

This feeling of fear, anger, loneliness came up in you many times in the past. They are your old friends. Breathing

Listen to **Walking Meditation to Embrace Your Emotions** at SoundsTrue.com/walkingmeditation/meditations.

in, stepping. "Hello, fear, anger, loneliness, my old friend." Breathing out, stepping, I smile to my old friend. In. "Hello, fear, anger, my old friend." Out. "Welcome back, I see you." In, my old friend, loneliness, fear is here. Out. I smile to my old friend. In. You are still there, my old friend, fear. Out. I see you, I am here for you.

At this point, you begin to recognize, to be in touch with your fear, your anger, your loneliness, and greet them as you greet your old friends, and smile to them. Acknowledge their presence in you by breathing in, stepping. By breathing out, stepping. Connecting with the Earth.

The next part of your practice is to continue to breathe with your belly as you step. Your hands are still on your chest. And, your emotion is there in your chest. Your fear is sitting there. Your anger, your loneliness is sitting there. You continue to breathe and walk.

And now, please do not think about anything else except resting on your breath, kissing the Earth with your feet. Breathing in, I know I am breathing in as my foot caresses the ground. Breathing out, I know I am breathing out as my foot kisses the ground.

Please, walk in this way, in the presence of your fear, of your anger, of your loneliness. They are sitting in your chest, they're resting there. Your breath and your step are cradling your pain and your fear. Your breaths and your steps are together creating a nest. A nest, a cradle around your baby of fear, your baby of pain, your baby of loneliness that is lying there in your chest.

Your baby of fear, your baby of pain, is very vulnerable and is crying very hard. Just let the baby rest in your chest. Please, try not to do anything to the baby. Respect the baby. Continue to walk and breathe with awareness so that you can create a warm nest for your baby. Walking in this way, breathing in this way, you become a tender, loving mother taking care of your crying baby of pain. You are all right because your baby is resting in your chest, in this cradle of mindfulness.

Breathing in, one step. Calming. Breathing out, one step. Resting. You rest. Your pain can rest. Your baby of fear can rest.

In. Out. In. Out. In. The baby may be still crying a little bit, it's OK. Tell her it's OK. Out. In. Out. In. Out.

Resting. Resting.

Cradling. Cradling.

Cradling. Cradling.

Breathing in, the baby of fear, the baby of anger in me is being cradled. The breath and the step are coming wonderfully together. Breathing out, the baby of fear in me is still being cradled. In. Cradling. Out. Cradling.

And gradually, you notice that the storm of fear, of

The First Noble Truth taught by the Buddha is the presence of suffering. Awareness of suffering generates compassion, and compassion generates the will to practice the Way.

When I returned to France after trying to help the boat people, life here seemed so strange. I had just seen refugees being robbed, raped, and killed at sea, while in Paris, the shops were filled with every kind of product and people were drinking coffee and wine under neon lights. It was like a dream. How could there be such discrepancies? Aware of the depth of suffering in the world, I vowed not to live superficially.

T.N.H.

anger, has begun to disappear. Breathing in, the storm of emotion is passing. Breathing out, it's passing. Breathing in, one step. The storm of fear is leaving. Breathing out, one step. The sky is becoming clearer and clearer.

Breathing in, the storm has gone. Breathing out, the sun begins to shine. In, the storm has disappeared. Out, I smile to the clear sky. In, clear sky. Out, smiling. In. Out. Breathing in, the storm of emotion is impermanent in nature. It comes, it stays for a while, and it goes. Breathing out, I smile to the impermanent nature of my emotions, of my fear, of my anger.

In the next few minutes, please continue to walk peacefully, relaxingly. Kissing the Earth. Enjoy kissing the Earth with every step you make. Feel as solid again as the Earth. Breathing in, solid Earth. Breathing out, I feel solid.

Please continue to enjoy your breathing.

When anger arises, walking meditation can be very helpful.
Try reciting this verse as you walk:

Breathing in, I know that anger is in me.
Breathing out, I know this feeling is unpleasant.

And then, after a while:

Breathing in, I feel calm.
Breathing out, I am now strong enough to take care
of this anger.

Until you are calm enough to look directly at the anger,
just enjoy your breathing, your walking, and the beauties
of the outdoors. After a while, the anger will subside
and you will feel strong enough to look directly at it, to
try to understand its causes, and to begin the work of
transforming it.   **THICH NHAT HANH**

If You Are Having Difficulty Practicing Walking Meditation to Embrace Your Emotions

If you experience a strong emotion and your heart begins to race and you cannot calm it down, or if you experience a lot of heat, tightening, or trembling in your body and belly breathing does not calm these symptoms, these are signs that you are not yet ready to walk with your emotions. It is best to follow the practice of calming and resting at this time, as explained in the chapters on conscious breathing and slow walking. Through continued practice of slow walking and walking in nature, the time will come when you will be able to directly cradle your pain or fear, and eventually understand its true nature.

Walk upright, with calm, dignity, and joy, as though you were an emperor. Place your foot on the Earth the way an emperor places his seal on a royal decree. A decree can bring happiness or misery. Your steps can do the same. If your steps are peaceful, the world will have peace. If you can make one peaceful step, then peace is possible.

T.N.H.

6

GOING FURTHER

We who have two legs can easily practice
walking meditation. We must not forget
to be grateful. We walk for ourselves,
and we walk for those who cannot walk.
We walk for all living beings—past, present,
and future. **THICH NHAT HANH**

Physical Pain and Walking Meditation

The purpose of walking meditation is to stop, rest, and heal. If you are experiencing physical pain and cannot walk, you can lie on your back, you can sit, or you can rest in any position as long as you can follow your breathing. By breathing mindfully, you can bring yourself to a state of unity of body and mind, you can truly rest, and healing can begin. The energy of mindfulness is the energy of love and tenderness, which brings calm and soothes pain, just as when someone massages tension from your shoulders or back.

Usually when we experience a difficult emotion or a physical pain, we ignore it, or we do something else so we do not have to face it. But when physical pain becomes unbearable, it calls for our attention. Whether you have physical or emotional pain, the process of working with it in walking meditation is exactly the same. When you practiced embracing your emotions during walking meditation, you learned how to recognize them, embrace them, accept them, and cradle them until their roots were revealed to you. In this case, once you have connected with your body through the practice of mindful breathing, you can smile to your body and say, "Breathing in, I am aware of my body. Breathing out, I smile to my body." And then you can say to yourself, "Breathing in, I notice there is pain in my shoulder. Breathing out, I allow my breath to move through my shoulder and soften it."

If you are experiencing physical pain, you can practice conscious breathing to help you recognize your pain for what it is. If you do not recognize your physical pain as a sensation of physical discomfort, it is likely that it will become something more than physical pain to you. The fear and anxiety that are often created around the physical pain will seep into other parts of your body and your psyche as well. For instance, when your body is not at peace, it will be difficult for you to talk to people with kindness and gentleness. The Buddha said that when an arrow strikes the body, a feeling of pain arises. But when a second arrow strikes at the same spot, the pain is not just doubled but it is many times greater. The second arrow represents our fear and the stories we have about our physical pain. These can make us suffer a great deal more than physical pain alone.

The war in Vietnam caused countless injuries to the minds and bodies of people on both sides. Many soldiers and civilians lost an arm or a leg, and now they cannot join their palms together to pay respects to the Buddha or practice walking meditation. Last year two such people came to our retreat center, and we had to find alternate ways for them to practice walking meditation. I asked each of them to sit in a chair, choose someone who was practicing walking meditation, and become one with him, following his steps in mindfulness. In this way, they made peaceful and serene steps together with their partners, even though they themselves could not walk. I saw tears of joy in their eyes.

T.N.H.

For example, a simple experience of tightness in the chest may not be enough to get our attention, but if we fear that we may have a stroke or a heart attack, we become overwhelmed. We may not know what to do, or we may do more than we need to. When the tightness becomes so bad that it calls for our attention, we may think, "Oh, I have pain in my chest." Then we may get scared and create stories about our pain, such as, "I am having a heart attack!" Who writes this story? Our fear.

But if you first notice there is some tightness in your chest, you can sense what is wrong before it becomes a larger problem. You can put your hand on your chest and smile as you breathe in and say, "Tightness is here in my chest." And when you breathe out, you can say, "I am working so hard, and not taking time to care for myself or my body." And then, breathing in, you can say, "Relax, relax. Soften. Soften, my beloved chest." As you breathe, you can allow your breath to move through the tightness. When you bring this energy of conscious breathing, tenderness, and love to your pain, it softens, it relaxes, and it calms down. It is still pain, but it is pain in just that one area. It does not color your view of your body or your psyche or your day. The moment you bring attention to your physical pain and take care of it, you will also bring more harmony, peace, and love into your body.

Jogging

You can apply mindfulness to everything, including jogging. The way to bring mindfulness into your jogging experience is to jog at a comfortable pace while still being able to count the number of steps you take with each breath. Because you are exercising when you jog, your breathing will be faster than when you walk, but you can usually coordinate it with your steps (especially if you are not listening to music). Just feel the flow of your breath and the contact between your feet and the Earth as you jog, and become aware of the nature around you. In this way, you can continue to jog and hear the acorns falling, see the squirrels chasing each other, and feel the warmth of the sun. By practicing mindful breathing while jogging, you will also feel calmer, and your mind will become clearer.

Although jogging can be quite pleasant, it does not replace slow walking meditation. Remember, whatever happens in your body is also happening in your mind. Therefore, jogging—even mindful jogging—can never slow down your mind to the same degree as slow walking meditation.

Walking with Someone Who Does Not Know Walking Meditation

If you walk with someone who does not know walking meditation and she is ready and willing to learn, you can share walking meditation instruction with her. If she has no interest in learning walking meditation, you cannot share formal walking meditation with her, but you can take her hand and walk with her and share the peace and joy of walking together.

In walking meditation with others, we refrain from talking in order to maintain awareness of our breathing and our steps, and to enjoy each other's company. But if we are walking with someone who is not used to being quiet, then from time to time we may need to acknowledge them with a look or a smile, or respond to something they say, because if we do not it can be very awkward. Try not to get carried away by the conversation so you can share the peace and joy of mindful walking. Your serenity and peace can help the other person be calmer and more present to the beauty around them.

Walking with Children

It can be a great joy to take the hand of a child and walk with him while practicing conscious breathing. You can share your practice with him, or attempt to bring him into the present moment, by saying things like, "Ah, the trees here are so green." But do not initiate conversation that can take him away from the present moment. Your energy of mindfulness allows a deeper connection between you and the child. Your peace and serenity have become his, and his joy has become yours. If you walk with a child and the child is very energetic and likes to run around, you can say, "Walk with me for a few minutes and then you can

A child is a
bell of mindfulness,
reminding us how
wonderful life is.

T.N.H.

run and play." That is what I did with our son when he was young. I would walk with him for a few minutes, and then he would look up at me and I would say, "Do you want to run? Then go ahead and run."

When you walk, you might like to take the hand of a child. She will receive your concentration and stability, and you will receive her freshness and innocence. From time to time, she may want to run ahead and then wait for you to catch up. A child is a bell of mindfulness, reminding us how wonderful life is.

At Plum Village, I teach the young people a simple verse to practice while walking: "Oui, oui, oui," as they breathe in, and, "Merci, merci, merci," as they breathe out. "Yes, yes, yes. Thanks, thanks, thanks." I want them to respond to life, to society, and to the Earth in a positive way. They enjoy it very much. **THICH NHAT HANH**

Experiencing Difficulties in the Family

It is best to practice walking meditation daily. It can be very unsettling if your family is experiencing a problem and you say "I'm going for a walk" and leave the situation. It is better if they are accustomed to your practice. And for your part, if you practice outdoor walking meditation every day, you will already be aware of how much fresher, happier, and more alive you are when you come back home. By practicing mindfulness regularly, you will bring more awareness and concentration to everything you do, and, because of that clarity, you will be able to gain greater understanding of who you and your loved ones truly are. This alone will help to improve the situation in your family. There will be fewer and less severe episodes of anger.

When Someone in Your Family Chooses Not to Practice Walking Meditation

When my husband and I practice walking meditation, we try to bring our loved ones with us. But we do not have expectations of our family members, and we do not get upset if they do not join us. When they cannot walk or they will not, we walk for them. A comment shared with me by many people is, "My partner does not practice. My children do not practice. I wish they would." And it is said as if the other person is at fault. Wishing the practice of walking meditation for your loved ones is good, but it can become an expectation that leads to disappointment and anger.

The best way to get your family members to begin walking meditation is to regularly practice yourself. As they see the benefits you gain from it, and as your relationship with them improves, they will be more inclined to begin the practice. It is not what you say but who you are that matters. If you think you are a better person than they are because you practice meditation and they do not, when you return home it will not be a rewarding experience for you or them. But if you walk primarily to calm yourself, to center yourself, to take care of yourself and the people you love, you will soon realize that the practice is not just for your own benefit. In the beginning you may come back from walking meditation and someone will start yelling at you and you may think, "How can you be like that? You are that way because you do not practice. You shatter my joy." But as you continue to practice, you will feel so nourished that you will have compassion for those who do not. You will not blame them for not practicing; instead, you will walk for them, you will smile for them, you will breathe for them. You may come back into the same situation, facing someone's anger, and think, "You're behaving like that? Okay, I will not get mad. You do not know the practice of breathing and smiling, my darling, but not to worry. I will walk for you."

If You Are Unable to Walk

Becoming one with another person's mindful walking allows you to share her experience. As you sit and watch the other person walk, you might like to coordinate your breathing with her steps. In this way, that person walks for you, you sit for her, and both of you are breathing together. But if there is no one with whom to practice mindful walking, you can close your eyes, relax, and consciously breathe, and visualize that you are making stable, peaceful steps among the trees and the flowers.

Walking for Our Ancestors

Your healing goes much deeper and farther through time and space than you can imagine. Walking and embracing your emotions brings healing not only to your heart but to the hearts of the ancestors you carry inside of you. Your parents, your grandparents, and all of your ancestors have transmitted not only their love and hope to you, but also the wounds in their hearts. The love, joy, fear, and anger that you are experiencing are not just yours, but also theirs. Once you are able to come home to your body, your mind, and your breath, you can feel the presence of your ancestors and touch their joy and love inside yourself very closely. When you can smile, they can smile. When you can take a peaceful, loving step, they can take a peaceful, loving step with you. When you can heal yourself, you will begin to heal them as well. And once the sources and nature of your wounds are understood and transformed, you will be able to transmit that understanding and healing to your children, your grandchildren, and future generations.

FINAL BLESSING

As you make the effort to let go of your worries and anxieties, please smile. It may be just the beginning of a smile, but keep it there on your lips. It is very much like the Buddha's half-smile. As you learn to walk as the Buddha walked, you can smile as he smiled. Why wait until you are completely transformed, completely awakened? You can start being a part-time Buddha right now!

The half-smile is the fruit of your awareness that you are here, alive, walking. At the same time, it nurtures more peace and joy within you. Smiling as you practice walking meditation will keep your steps calm and peaceful, and give you a deep sense of ease. A smile refreshes your whole being and strengthens your practice. Don't be afraid to smile. **THICH NHAT HANH**

Now that you have learned the art of mindful walking to nourish peace, joy, compassion, and gratitude with every step, may a fresh breeze rise with each step as you walk. May you continue to nurture yourself and others with the peace, understanding, compassion, and joy that you have cultivated from the practice of mindful breathing and mindful walking. May flowers bloom beneath your feet.

Let us walk with our loved ones. Let us walk for those who are in prisons, for those who are in wheelchairs or on crutches, for those who cannot take gentle, peaceful steps because of the tremendous amount of suffering in their hearts. Let us hold their hands as we walk with them and for them.

Walking mindfully on the Earth can restore our peace and harmony, and it can restore the Earth's peace and harmony as well. We are children of the Earth. We rely on her for our happiness, and she relies on us. Whether the Earth is beautiful, fresh, and green, or arid and parched, depends on our way of walking. When we practice walking meditation beautifully, we massage the Earth with our feet and plant seeds of joy and happiness with each step. Our Mother will heal us, and we will heal her.

Each Step

Through the deserted gate,
full of ripened leaves,
I follow the small path.
Earth is as red as a child's lips.
Suddenly
I am aware
of each step
I make.

T.N.H.

FURTHER RESOURCES

Learn more about the work of Nguyen Anh-Huong

Mindfulness Practice Center of Fairfax
Telephone: 703.938.1377
Email: info@mpcf.org
mpcf.org

Learn more about the work of Thich Nhat Hanh

Plum Village: plumvillage.org (information, teachings, and retreats)

Parallax Press: parallax.org (books, audios, and videos)

Attending Mindfulness Retreats

To deepen your practice, it is highly recommended that, at some point, you attend a mindfulness retreat that offers teachings and practice on walking meditation as presented here. The collective energy of mindfulness at a retreat is so powerful that it will be much easier for you to succeed in the art of mindful walking.

For information on attending a mindfulness or walking meditation retreat with Nguyen Anh-Huong, please contact the Mindfulness Practice Center of Fairfax at mpcf.org.

For information on attending meditation retreats with Thich Nhat Hanh in the United States, France, and Vietnam, please visit his website at plumvillage.org.

NGUYEN ANH-HUONG

is one of the first students ordained as a dharma teacher
by Thich Nhat Hanh. She has taught mindfulness practices
across the United States since 1988.

THICH NHAT HANH

is a Zen master in the Vietnamese tradition, scholar, poet,
and peace activist. He is the author of the national bestseller
Living Buddha, Living Christ and over sixty other books.

ABOUT SOUNDS TRUE

Sounds True is a multimedia publisher whose mission is to inspire and support personal transformation and spiritual awakening. Founded in 1985 and located in Boulder, Colorado, we work with many of the leading spiritual teachers, thinkers, healers, and visionary artists of our time. We strive with every title to preserve the essential "living wisdom" of the author or artist. It is our goal to create products that not only provide information to a reader or listener, but that also embody the quality of a wisdom transmission.

For those seeking genuine transformation, Sounds True is your trusted partner. At SoundsTrue.com you will find a wealth of free resources to support your journey, including exclusive weekly audio interviews, free downloads, interactive learning tools, and other special savings on all our titles.

To learn more, please visit SoundsTrue.com/freegifts or call us toll-free at 800.333.9185.

Printed in the USA
CPSIA information can be obtained
at www.ICGtesting.com
LVHW070722010324
773128LV00004B/463